W9-CJX-937

A VERMONT 14

A Map of the STATE of VERMONT by J. Whitelaw 1795

A VERMONT 14

COMMEMORATIVE OF THE
TWO-HUNDREDTH ANNIVERSARY OF
VERMONT'S ADMISSION TO THE UNION AS
THE NATION'S FOURTEENTH STATE

1791–1991

Edited by

EDWARD CONNERY LATHEM
and VIRGINIA L. CLOSE

BURLINGTON
University of Vermont Libraries

1992

LIBRARY
COLBY-SAWYER COLLEGE
NEW LONDON, NH 03257

OVER
F
49
.V53
1992

25836273

Principal sponsorship of this volume
has been provided through a grant from

THE WILLIAM L. BRYANT FOUNDATION

supplemented by a contribution from

NATHAN S. ANCELL

*Founder & Chairman Emeritus
of Ethan Allen Incorporated*

as well as by a corporate gift from

ETHAN ALLEN INCORPORATED

*headquartered at Danbury, Connecticut, and
having among its manufacturing facilities
plants located within the state of Vermont,
a firm bearing the name of Vermont's famous
soldier-author-farmer-statesman who died
at Burlington in 1789, two years before
Vermont attained its U.S. statehood*

The provision of copies for complimentary
distribution to libraries in Vermont has
been made possible by funds contributed by

THE WINDHAM FOUNDATION

FRONTISPIECE Topographic representation dating from
the period two years after Vermont's attainment of U.S. statehood: James Whitelaw's 1793 "A Map of the State of Vermont,"
engraved at Boston by Callender for inclusion as a fold-out
frontispiece in Samuel Williams' *The Natural and Civil History
of Vermont* (Walpole, New Hampshire: Isaiah Thomas & David
Carlisle Jun., 1794). [Reproduced in slight reduction from a
copy in the Dartmouth College Library.]

1/0/04

FEATURED within this volume are fourteen publications—publications that span a period of just over two centuries and variously relate to America's fourteenth state. Although the selection includes works that do qualify as Vermontiana of classic or of landmark character, some of the components have been chosen on the basis of their simply providing representation of certain different kinds of resources or different areas of subject matter, but without an attempt to achieve anything approaching a comprehensiveness of coverage in that regard. The authors who have contributed the commentaries that are presented herein have produced texts treating of and extending from the individual publications which together constitute this garland of historical commemoration and of tribute.

December 1991

1

Eden Burroughs

*A Sincere Regard
to Righteousness and Piety*

1778

A SINCERE REGARD TO RIGHTEOUSNESS AND
PIETY, THE SOLE MEASURE OF A TRUE PRIN-
CIPLE OF HONOR AND PATRIOTISM.

ILLUSTRATED IN

A

SERMON,

PREACHED BEFORE HIS EXCELLENCY THE
GOVERNOR,
THE HONORABLE COUNCIL,
AND HOUSE OF REPRESENTATIVES,
IN THE STATE OF

VERMONT,

OCTOBER 8th, A. D. 1778.

By EDEN BURROUGHS, *A. M.*
Pastor of the Church in *Hanover.*

DRESDEN, State of *VERMONT:*
Printed by J. P. & A. SPOONER,
Printers to the GENERAL ASSEMBLY of said State.

THERE EXISTS a degree of irony in the circumstance that Vermont's earliest printing was in fact done on the eastern side, not the west side, of the Connecticut River—thus being, in a sense, of New Hampshire origin, even though proclaiming itself to have been produced at "Dresden, State of Vermont."

What was involved, by way of historical context, reaches back to the granting of townships in what is now Vermont—grants made, beginning in the mid-18th Century, by New Hampshire's royal governor, Benning Wentworth. The legality of such grants was vigorously challenged by the Province of New York, which long had claimed that area as territory under its jurisdiction.

Conflict and controversy ensued. Then, in 1764 an order issued by King George III established that the far bank of the Connecticut River should be New Hampshire's western boundary. (And one substantive effect of this has been, it may be noted, that New Hampshire ends up paying ninety percent of the costs of all bridges across the Connecticut. An example of Vermont shrewdness—from a period even before Vermont had actually come into being!)

In the wake of the royal decree, further turmoil occurred when New York officials proceeded to dispossess New Hampshire grantees and to reassign their property to others. The rancorous dispute was interrupted—at least in part—by the outbreak of the Revolutionary War.

But the coming of American independence brought about conditions within the Province of New Hampshire that were also to contribute, in a significant fashion, to the creation of a State of Vermont. This occurred when a number of New Hampshire towns, along or not far removed from the east side of the Connecticut River, believed themselves to have been maltreated in terms of representation accorded them within New Hampshire's Provincial Congress.

Feeling aggrieved, over a dozen of these towns concluded to ally themselves with towns beyond the river, which had in 1777 joined in setting up an independent, sovereign government—at first called New Connecticut, then promptly renamed Vermont. And among the New Hampshire towns accepted in 1778 into union with Vermont was one that had in fact been a town for less than a month's time: Dresden, consisting of those parts of Hanover and of neighboring Lebanon located contiguous to Dartmouth College.

The fledgling Vermont republic was to experience many vicissitudes, relating to such questions as how (if indeed at all) it should be constituted, and centering, too, upon just where the eastern border of New York State should be. But when in 1781 the Continental Congress refused to consider recognition of Vermont until it abandoned claims to land or citizenry regarded at Philadelphia as properly belonging to either New Hampshire or New York, the die was cast for Vermont ultimately to become—a decade later and essentially bounded as it is today—a member of the United States of America, this nation's fourteenth state.

It was a New Hampshire institution, Dartmouth College, that provided the means of Vermont's having its first imprints. In 1778 the college succeeded in luring to Hanover (or to what was then, temporarily, Dresden) a printer from Connecticut, and among the earliest of the today-known issuances of the Dresden press is Eden Burroughs's sermon entitled *A Sincere Regard to Righteousness and Piety, the Sole Measure of a True Principle of Honor and Patriotism*, a publication running to some thirty pages.

The Reverend Mr. Burroughs's message had a threefold objective, as the minister himself specified: "I. To shew what the wise man means by the righteousness which exalteth a nation. II. Point out the reasons why this righteousness will exalt a nation. III. Conclude with those addresses that will naturally arise out of my subject."

It is undoubtedly the case that we, today, would do well to heed what was so earnestly imparted to the members of Vermont's government on October 8th, A.D. 1778, and which caused the General Assembly to vote, in appreciation, to secure from its author "a Copy for the Press."

Thus it was that New Hampshire, at Hanover (or Dresden), brought the printed word to Vermont and inaugurated the state's literature, a kind and generous act that has been followed over the years by other benevolence (reaching a height of graciousness perhaps when we "lent" Vermont our poet, Robert Frost—who wrote, it will be remembered, after he moved from the White Mountain region to that of the Green: "It's restful . . . just to think about New Hampshire. / At present I am living in Vermont.").

But what, in closing, can be said of Dresden, the town that had not been a town at all until partitioned into being in 1778? Its existence, as has already been suggested, was of short duration. Within the span of a half-dozen years the domain was returned to the two municipalities from which it had initially been carved—with Dartmouth College, accordingly, restored to having a Hanover, New Hampshire, address.

However, the name Dresden is still in use, for in 1963, through a compact between Norwich, Vermont, and Hanover (as sanctioned by the legislatures of both states involved and by the United States Congress), there was established the Dresden School District, as an instrument for jointly conducting education in grades seven through twelve—something that was at its inception this country's only such educational authority spanning the borders of two states.

Association and interplay—typically co-operative and constructive, although on occasion purposefully competitive—have existed between New Hampshire and Vermont for well over two centuries. It is, therefore, particularly gratifying for me to have an opportunity to salute Vermont, most warmly, on the occasion of the celebration of its 1791–1991 bicentennial.

JUDD GREGG
Governor of New Hampshire

His Excellency Governor Gregg having within the foregoing statement extended special bicentennial greetings to Vermont from the area immediately east of the Connecticut River, WE THE UNDERSIGNED, acting on behalf of the citizens of the Commonwealth, the State, and the Province that border Vermont to the south, the west, and the north, highly value this opportunity to join in New Hampshire's salute, by tendering a further expression of neighborly felicitation, cordial regard, and good wishes.

WILLIAM F. WELD
Governor, Commonwealth of Massachusetts

MARIO M. CUOMO
Governor, State of New York

ROBERT BOURASSA
Prime Minister, Province of Quebec

2

Laws of the
State of Vermont

1808

THE

LAWS

OF

THE STATE

OF

VERMONT,

DIGESTED AND COMPILED:

INCLUDING THE

DECLARATION OF INDEPENDENCE,

THE

CONSTITUTION OF THE UNITED STATES,

AND OF THIS STATE.

VOLUMES FIRST AND SECOND, COMING DOWN TO, AND INCLUDING THE
YEAR MDCCCVII; WITH AN *APPENDIX*, CONTAINING TITLES OF
LOCAL ACTS; AND AN *INDEX* OF THE *LAWS IN FORCE*.

PUBLISHED BY ORDER OF THE LEGISLATURE.

VOL. I.

RANDOLPH:
PRINTED BY SERENO WRIGHT,
PRINTER TO THE STATE.

1808.

ONLY four of our nation's fifty states—Vermont, Texas, California, and Hawaii—were, prior to their admission to the Union, completely independent, sovereign nations. Vermont was never a party to the Articles of Confederation and remained independent of the original thirteen states from January of 1777 to March of 1791.

The Vermont state constitution, adopted in 1777, has long been celebrated for its emphasis on individual rights. This emphasis is manifested in such provisions as the express prohibition of slavery, which appears in the state constitution's very first article, and the guarantee of universal manhood suffrage without regard to property ownership or financial means. Like other American colonists of that era, the citizens of Vermont were chiefly concerned with safeguarding their liberties from government infringement.

The state constitution provided that the Vermont General Assembly should consist of "persons most noted for wisdom and virtue, to be chosen by ballot by the freemen of every town." The first sessions of the General Assembly, held in March, June, and October of 1778, were devoted to the adoption of a set of laws for the state. No copies of those enactments appear to have survived, although it is reported that, as a temporary measure, one of the laws proclaimed that the laws of the state would be the laws "as they stand in the Connecticut law book, and in defect of those laws the plain word of God ascertained in the scriptures, . . . until the legislature should have time to digest and enact a code adapted to the condition of the country."

A printed edition of the 1782 *Revised Laws* was issued, followed approximately five years later by *Statutes of the State of Vermont, Passed by the Legislature in February and March 1787*, a volume that has been characterized as "probably the first complete body of permanent law enacted by . . . [Vermont] and published by authority." Today both of these publications are great rarities.

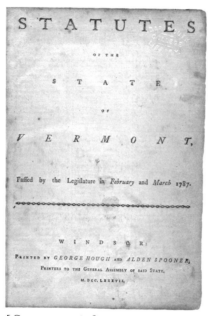

[*Statutes*, 1787]

A further revision of the state's laws was adopted by the General Assembly in 1797, and a published edition of that revision appeared in 1798, but it was not until 1807 — some sixteen years after Vermont was admitted to the Union — that the state authorized its first comprehensive compilation of laws, duly published the next year in two large octavo volumes.

As the title page of Volume I reflects, the 1808 edition, which ran to well over a thousand pages, contained the Declaration of Independence, the federal and state constitutions, and, of course, the Vermont statutes.

The compiler of the 1808 edition, Thomas Tolman, was an individual worthy of note. While still living in his native Massachusetts, Tolman enlisted in the Continental Army immediately after the Battle of Lexington in 1775, and thereafter served in different campaigns during the Revolutionary War, rising in rank to lieutenant. Upon moving to Vermont, he held a variety of elective and appointive offices and served as, among other things, secretary to Vermont's first governor, Thomas Chittenden, and the executive council.

The foregoing provides only a brief sketch of some of the events and developments associated with the early legal history of Vermont.

The citizens of Vermont still take "The Freeman's Oath," which requires them formally to pledge, "Whenever I give my vote or suffrage, touching any matter that concerns the State of Vermont, I will do it so as in my conscience I shall judge will most conduce to the best good of the same, as established by the Constitution, without fear or favor of any person." Implicit in this oath is the respect for the rule of law that the sons and daughters of the state have long shared. As John Greenleaf Whittier declared in his poem "The Song of the Vermonters 1779":

> Yet we owe no allegiance; we bow to no throne;
> Our ruler is law, and the law is our own;
> Our leaders themselves are our own fellow-men,
> Who can handle the sword, or the scythe, or the pen.

WARREN E. BURGER
Chief Justice of the United States 1969–87

3

The Green-Mountain
Songster

1823

THE

GREEN-MOUNTAIN SONGSTER,

BEING A COLLECTION OF

SONGS

ON VARIOUS SUBJECTS.

Principally tending to expel melancholy and cheer the drooping mind.

—∞—

BY AN OLD REVOLUTIONARY SOLDIER.

[Copy-Right secured.]

1823

THE title of *The Green-Mountain Songster* may have been chosen to identify its compiler, an "old Revolutionary soldier," as a Vermonter and a singer of songs. Much more likely, however, it identified the little book itself as a *songster*, a popular genre among early-American publications.

Songsters were anthologies of secular song texts, to be sung to tunes known to everyone. Hence, they rarely included actual music, though many suggested by name the tunes to which the lyrics were to be sung: "Yankee Doodle," "Derry Down," "God Save Great Washington," and the like. Most songsters were small—literally pocket books; and most of their compilers chose anonymity.

American songsters had begun to appear in the 1730s, the first one (a Masonic tract with a song-text supplement) having been printed by Benjamin Franklin. At first, they aped English songsters and, indeed, contained mostly British poems—the lyrics of sheet music or of songs in such huge (and expensive) collections as Thomas d'Urfey's *Wit and Mirth; or, Pills to Purge Melancholy*. Later, American songsters were more topical, reflecting the changing political scene—as do *Loyal and Humorous Songs* (1779) and *Liberty Songs* (1785)—with reworkings of English lyrics and brand-new American ones. *The Green-Mountain Songster* exemplifies the sub-genre of the "ballad songster," with its large proportion of storytelling ballads of the sort later gathered so assiduously by song collectors such as Francis Child in the 19th Century, and in this century Vermont's own Helen Hartness Flanders.

The Green-Mountain Songster was neither the first nor the last of Vermont's contributions to the enormous tide of American songsters—some 650 having been published here before 1821. (The Bennington printer Anthony Haswell had brought out *The Little Scholar's Pretty Pocket Companion* in 1795 and went on to issue seven more songsters by 1809.) But our Green-Mountain book is unique as a compilation by one who, though remaining anonymous, reveals himself as an avid and appreciated singer.

On his title page the Unknown Soldier of Sandgate (the preface is signed and dated as having been written at that Bennington County place) promises a collection of lyrics "on various subjects" and principally ones "tending to expel melancholy and cheer the drooping mind." His preface expands on that theme:

"... Most people are fond of singing. Good moral cheerful songs are useful to cheer the drooping mind. The author has experienced this when called upon to sing where people have been afflicted in their minds, and [are] sinking into melancholy. ..."

But our "Revolutionary soldier" was dubious about the political efficacy of songs:

"... A song is but a song at any rate. Some seem to side

with France and some with England, but France and England are old powers and can take care of themselves—every tub should stand on its own bottom. . . . Let us subdue all our political animosities, and meet, presenting to one another the OLIVE BRANCH of peace, and unite. . . ."

Following this genial admonition comes a collection of almost fifty lyrics. Many are British ballads, but there are also tales of the New World, such as "General Wolfe," "The Capture of the Macedonian" (a British frigate taken in the War of 1812), and "Joel Baker" (a youth from Alstead, just across the Connecticut River from Bellows Falls, who, an inconsolably unrequited lover, committed suicide). Poems other than ballads include "Washington and Jefferson" (one hero dead, the other a worthy successor); "Adam and Eve" (a homily on bundling: ". . . Ruth is beguil'd and got with child who bundling did refuse"); and "The Liberty Song" (". . . Unite, unite, Americans, with purse, with heart and hand, / Divided we shall surely fall, united we shall stand").

Only one copy of *The Green-Mountain Songster* is known. This indicates, not that it was issued in very few copies, and those mostly discarded, but that it was immensely popular, its copies worn out with use. A songster was an everyday, utilitarian object, not a prized heirloom. In a time when almost all Americans were just plain folks, its songs were not "folksongs," but just plain songs. It opens wide the doors to understanding the pleasures and pains, the ideas and ideals of early America.

H. WILEY HITCHCOCK
President, American Musicological Society

4

Daniel Pierce Thompson

The Green Mountain Boys

1839

THE

GREEN MOUNTAIN BOYS:

A

HISTORICAL TALE

OF THE EARLY SETTLEMENT OF VERMONT.

BY THE

AUTHOR OF 'MAY MARTIN, OR THE MONEY DIGGERS.'

Thompson, Daniel Pierce

"'T is a rough land of rock, and stone, and tree,
Where breathes no castled lord, nor cabin'd slave:
Where thoughts, and hands, and tongues are free,
And friends will find a welcome—foes a grave."

IN TWO VOLUMES.

VOL. I.

MONTPELIER:
E. P. WALTON AND SONS, PUBLISHERS AND PRINTERS.
1839.

D A N I E L Pierce Thompson described his great novel *The Green Mountain Boys* as "a historical tale." To the present-day historian, the story reads as a romantic and one-sided recapitulation of events. But it constitutes a wonderful parable of the Revolutionary period.

Written two generations after the start of armed conflict with Britain, the novel (initially published in 1839 in a two-volume edition) participated in constructing the myths and legends by which the new nation wished to be known. In its pages one can see the author shaping images about our past—images that would shape the future. His success can be gauged by the book's popularity. It is said to have been reprinted fifty times before 1860 and another ten by 1900.

The plot of the novel recalls the birth of these United States, and especially the struggle for liberty out of which the State of Vermont emerged. Plucky frontiersmen and women who have cleared the forest with their own hard labor struggle to maintain their holdings, against the depredations of greedy New York land jobbers and the Crown that supported them. Defending their land, the denizens of the frontier are not only defending their families, but they are also defending honor, honest toil, and the collective will of the country folk, against greed, corruption, and the misuse of Indians.

Virtue is rewarded in the end, by marriage: the union of

two young women, whose fathers had served the British army, with two brave officers of the Green Mountain regiments signals the creation of a new American family.

The modern reader will recoil at some of the stereotypes in which Thompson indulges. He depicts Indians as lazy scavengers unwilling to do regular work, and African-Americans as easily duped. Women fall into recognizable patterns: the young and innocent have calm, trim demeanors and act the part of obedient and blushing daughters; mothers are protective and loving, willing to sacrifice even their lives for their children. In a memorable phrase, Thompson describes a man's wife as "his loving rib."

The novel's seamless division between innocence and virtue, on the one hand, and evil, on the other, extends to its protagonists the qualities that Thompson hopes his readers will absorb. Vermont's rebels are denizens of nature. Familiar with its woods and streams, they use trees, caves, rivers, and cliffs to protect themselves. Fearing nothing from these natural haunts, they adopt the qualities of the courageous. They are sturdy and high-minded gentlemen, comely and generous fellows. They punish their opponents fairly, behaving more like "merry pranksters" than men determined on their rights. We are told they are so good that children instinctively gravitate to them.

In contrast, their opponents are sly and base fellows, capable of low and despicable plottings. They lie and steal, even from those who trust them; they would not hesitate to deprive a widow of her home, and leave her children helpless, or to violate a woman's honor.

The lessons of these sharp divisions cannot have been lost on Thompson's contemporaries. In this conflict between good and evil, authority is often contested, but there is little question that right must win. Thus, Benedict Arnold gives in readily to Ethan Allen's greater claim to command his troops. The "Yorkers" must lose their rights to the lands earned by the sweated labor of New Hampshire settlers. The followers of the paths of evil are blown to smithereens by gunpowder, without the loss of a single virtuous life. And in the end, the British, despite their greater numbers and superior arms, cannot prevail against the justice of the American cause.

Thompson wrote from the perspective of a politically active lawyer and judge, in a period when corruption was rife and many feared that the claims of nature would be sacrificed to the increasingly insistent demands of cities, banks, and incipient corporations. Eager to find an alternative to the spirit of greed he saw all around, he relied heavily on the memories of old-timers, to engage his readers in a spirit of patriotism. *The Green Mountain Boys* exemplified his love for traditional values as they were embodied in the easier choices of a simpler time.

For Thompson, the lessons of history were embodied in the efforts of a few brave men and virtuous women to stand fast to the values in which they believed. This is more than great romance; it is a lesson we cannot afford to ignore.

ALICE KESSLER-HARRIS
President, American Studies Association

5

Fairbanks' Patent
Platform & Counter Scales

1847

FAIRBANKS'

PATENT

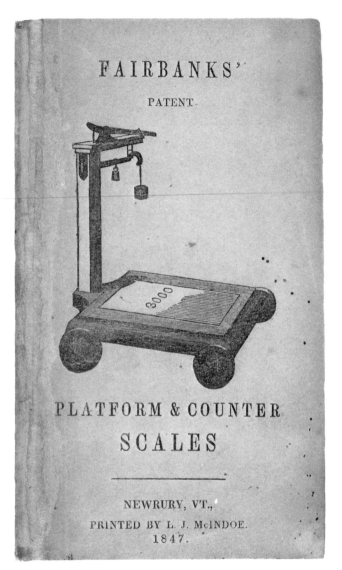

PLATFORM & COUNTER
SCALES

NEWRURY, VT.,
PRINTED BY L. J. McINDOE.
1847.

[Front cover]

[Opening page]

FAIRBANKS'
PATENT PLATFORM AND COUNTER
SCALES.

MANUFACTURED BY

E. & T. FAIRBANKS & CO.

ST. JOHNSBURY, VERMONT.

(*For List of Agents, see pages*, 18, 19, 20.)

ALTHOUGH industriousness has traditionally been held to be a characteristic of Vermonters, the word "industrial" has but limited application in any description of the state's economy.

Manufacturing and industry have, over the years, indeed existed and flourished in Vermont, even notably so. E. & T. Fairbanks & Co. (whose 1847 catalogue is pictured here) is an example—a firm that developed an international business at St. Johnsbury, based on the inventiveness of Thaddeus Fairbanks, who in 1831 patented the first platform scale. And one could also cite such enterprises as quarrying at Barre and Proctor, machine-tool making in Springfield, insurance at Montpelier and Burlington, and much else.

But some three decades ago, after a dozen or more years of summer residence in Southeastern Vermont, I became aware of another important source of revenue for and economic support to the state's economy. That was from what I called "The Pleasures and Uses of Bankruptcy." Those so contributing, I argued, add greatly to the comfort, convenience, and pleasure of country life and may even make it tolerable. They are the people who systematically disburse their savings, money they have inherited, or whatever they can borrow, on enterprises conducted for the public good. They grow things, make useful articles, or—most important of all—render valuable services that one could never obtain on a purely commercial basis. Their prices are not always low, but since they are always selling below cost, no one can complain. The community benefits not only from the goods and services they supply, but also from the rent or interest they pay, the purchases they make, and the payrolls they meet.

To be sure, the day comes when the rent, interest, bills, and payroll become troublesome or can no longer be met. But, invariably, others then come along. The competition to serve the public at a loss is rather keen. In a town not far from our house in Vermont is an inn which has failed decisively in the financial sense not once, but twice in the past five years. It is now up for sale at the highest price yet. The chances of getting what is asked or something close are excellent. On the basis of this and other cases, it is my belief that service generally improves with each bankruptcy.

Inns provide the best example of capital consumption, to give this admirable Vermont phenomenon its technical name. In the course of an autumn holiday, to offer what economists call a synthetic model of reality, a man and his wife from New Canaan take a leisurely motor trip to Montreal. They are fond of the country, which is why they live in Fairfield County and why they chose this particular trip. Somewhere between Brattleboro and Montpelier they spend a night at a village inn on a secondary road—not a motel, but the real thing, with maples all but hiding the small Shell station across the way. What peace! What a contrast between the life of the innkeepers and their own! Independence and serenity as against the daily penance of commuting, the obscene struggle on the subway, and the crushing pressures of organization.

The travelers have talked of getting out of the rat race. Could it really happen? It won't happen to many people, but it could happen to them. This husband has about fifteen years before actuarial decrepitude, the sense to know it, and a keen desire to enjoy the years that remain. His wife is younger and a good companion. They have some money. They have something even more precious, which is imagination and courage and a knowledge of how to cook.

Vaguely, perhaps more than vaguely, they know that the trend is away from the great corporations. The small entrepreneur has always been morally superior—a true child of freedom. Even liberal Democrats support him to the hilt. He is especially esteemed by the business journals which regularly publish vignettes of small-business ingenuity, enterprise, and success. Quite a number of them tell of men who found fulfillment and success by starting out on their own very late in life. None tells of failure. Those of us who profit from the savings of people who are going broke are profoundly indebted to these and similar success stories and the overtones of community stature, moral fiber, social responsibility, and easy money which they contain. The couple returns to the village and searches out the real-estate man. He is not hard to find.

"Yes, there is a good small inn for sale." It turns out to be the one at which they stopped. This is no coincidence; nearly all small country inns are for sale. Being from New York and, therefore, experienced in the tools of modern management, the husband has a good hard look at the books. He finds that it has been losing money. Perceptively and quite correctly, he attributes the losses to bad management. What he does not know is that such enterprises never make enough money to give the impression even of indifferent management.

So, the previous owners go back to New Jersey. For four years they have furnished jobs and modest wages to the community. They have bought meat and frozen vegetables from the local grocer and quite a bit of liquor from the state store. There were moments when it seemed possible that the liquor might put them in the black and other less commercial interludes when it eased toil and softened anxiety. The part-time residents* have had a place with atmosphere and home cooking at which to dine and, on occasion, to deposit a redundant guest. During the two-week deer season and the week before Labor Day, business was always amazing—several times what could be accommodated.

Because of the competition to serve, the previous owners

---

*On the whole, we would rather be called "part-time residents" than "summer people" because, as compared with Maine or Martha's Vineyard, we arrive earlier in the summer and stay much later in the autumn, so we are really part of the community.

are selling out at a considerable capital gain. They have also provided the regular residents with considerable unpaid labor, although it is the capital that really counts.

The future is also bright. The local carpenter and his two men can look forward to the busiest autumn since another couple from New Jersey converted their barn into a full-time furniture factory, for the new owners of the inn have unhesitantly identified better management with modernizing the kitchen, refurnishing the bedrooms, adding two baths, and making the former woodshed into a cozy new bar. These improvements will make the inn a better place to leave or take guests and more of an all-round community asset.

Lest anyone think this story contrived, let me return to strict matters of experience. For some years, we have been eating meals at a succession of inns that were being endowed by their owners. The owners were from the city. All were able to bring a modest amount of capital to our service. We always guessed that they were spending money on us, and this could have meant—there are some subtle differences here between average and marginal costs—that each visit absorbed some of their capital. Nonetheless, we always felt that our patronage was a real favor and so did they. We were always sorry to see them go, as eventually they did, but we were comforted by the knowledge that others would take their place, and others always have.

Until last year, our plumbing was done by a man from Long Island, who left suddenly for, I believe, Montana. We

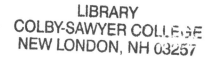
LIBRARY
COLBY-SAWYER COLLEGE
NEW LONDON, NH 03257

110104

have some excellent and very inexpensive furniture from a former furniture factory. I owe a dollar and fifty cents for some white gladioli to a man who disappeared before I could pay him. A nice neighbor left his job in New York to drill artesian wells; we would have patronized him, but unhappily he went out of business just before we ran out of water.

Some time ago, I negotiated for a piece of property with a former army colonel who had left his job on Wall Street to enter the local real-estate business. When I suggested that the price was too high, he said I had mortally insulted his professional honor as a West Pointer, and the deal fell through. He is now back in a bond house. We used to sell our hay to a horse farm which provided an excellent market while it lasted. We get firewood from people—they change frequently—who believe that their forest is a real resource. The list of such benefactors could be extended almost indefinitely.

The notion of an economic system in which everyone works hard, saves his money, and then disperses it by running useful enterprises for the common good is very attractive. However, the local Vermonters do not participate to any extent. They have a strong preference for profitable activity. This means they are rarely to be found running country inns, making furniture, growing African violets (an especially imaginative current venture), or raising horses or growing potatoes. U.S. Route 5 makes its way along the eastern border of the state, through a hideous neon-lighted tunnel walled by motels, antique stores, roadside furniture shops featuring not Vermont, but North Carolina craftsmanship, and, of course, service stations and restaurants. There are no New Yorkers, only Vermonters, on Route 5. One can hardly trade the rat race for a multiple-lane highway.

As a nation, we owe much to subsidies. They built the railroads, and also the airlines. Advocates of protection have never wavered in their belief that it was tariff subsidies—as distinct from, say, unduly free competition—that made our country industrially great. Our merchant marine is kept afloat by a subsidy, and also our banking system. Evidently, therefore, we need feel no shame that our pleasant Vermont countryside is subsidized by aspiring small enterprisers. And as subsidies go, this is an excellent one. Unlike farm support prices, it requires no federal appropriations and brings no charges that we are living too well at the taxpayers' expense. Unlike the depletion allowances enjoyed by the oilmen, it brings no complaints, quite justified, of fantastic favoritism.

Our subsidy is perfectly reliable, for, as I have noted, when one entrepreneur has exhausted his capital and credit, another is always ready and eager to take his place. The very best journals proclaim the virtue of such sacrifice on our behalf. It is a demonstration of worth, an affirmation of faith in the system. A recession or depression increases the number of people seeking the serenity of the country and the security of their own business. The outlays must have a certain cogency to the individuals involved, but this has nothing to do with the great impersonal sweep of economic forces.

JOHN KENNETH GALBRAITH
Teacher, Author, Diplomat

6

Abby Maria Hemenway

The Vermont Gazetteer

1867–1891

THE

VERMONT

HISTORICAL GAZETTEER:

A Magazine,

EMBRACING

A HISTORY OF EACH TOWN,

CIVIL, ECCLESIASTICAL, BIOGRAPHICAL AND MILITARY.

EDITED BY

ABBY MARIA HEMENWAY.

IN THREE VOLUMES.

VOLUME I.
ADDISON, BENNINGTON, CALEDONIA, CHITTENDEN AND ESSEX COUNTIES.

——∞◦◦§◦◦∞——

Burlington, Vt:
PUBLISHED BY MISS A. M. HEMENWAY.
1867.

ABBY Maria Hemenway would have considered the inclusion of her *Vermont Historical Gazetteer* within this commemorative volume to be heartening recognition of the achievement of her life's goal. In the preface to one of her volumes, she declared, addressing herself to Vermont friends who had supported and sustained her endeavors, "as a daughter of Vermont, there is nothing . . . we would as soon have been as your historiographer."

The impetus for Miss Hemenway's undertaking of her ambitious endeavor was a realization "that our historic material is becoming—and will continue to become—daily more and more indistinct and irrecoverable," as well as a conviction "that our past has been too rich and, in many points, or some, too unique and romantic to lose. . . ."

Taking on the capacity of its editor and publisher herself, she launched in 1860 the *Vermont Quarterly Magazine*, devoted to writings on local history "gathered . . . as thoroughly and completely as they could be in each town now, and arranged in a series by counties." The individual numbers ultimately were to be incorporated "into two or more large volumes . . . which would be of permanent interest and utility."

Quarterly issuance of the publication proved, however, to be infeasible. Its first six numbers appeared at irregular intervals during the period 1860–63. Then, as Miss Hemenway

later recounted, "the work not receiving financial support sufficient to sustain it during war-days," it was suspended until
the Civil War had ended. Finally, "peace and prosperity being
established once more," five further numbers were brought
forth, as a unit, in 1867; and this, in turn, provided the basis
for gathering all eleven of the existing parts into a single fat
Volume I, carrying the title page here displayed. Thereafter,
no attempt at quarterly publishing was pursued.

Although the title page of the initial volume reflects the
intention or expectation that completion of the overall project
would require but three volumes, actually, there followed four
more: in 1871, 1877, 1882, and (posthumously, for Abby Maria
Hemenway died in February of 1890) in 1891—totalling approximately six thousand pages and, it has been estimated,
some four million words. But, even then, one volume remained
unfinished—that meant to cover Windsor County.

The contents of the *Vermont Historical Gazetteer* depended on contributions from citizens from each of the towns
in the state, and Miss Hemenway—all too successful in her
gathering process—tried to include *everything* she received.
Some realization of the scope and detailed nature of what was
put by her between covers, in printed and bound form, can be
derived from the fact that an index, prepared for the five-vol-
ume set and published in 1923, runs to 982 double-columned
pages of names and to another 134 pages citing subject entries.

Miss Hemenway produced a monument—one that was
achieved with extraordinary dedication and, even, despite

privation. As we now look upon her legacy, it provides an opportunity for comment on the importance of local history for today's citizens and societies.

Carol Kammen, in her 1986 book *On Doing Local History*, asserts: "Local history is, at its heart—as is history itself—the study of the human condition in and through time. We look for an understanding of our past." She also notes that there are many and varied forms of history and of historical methods encompassed by local history—something Miss Hemenway instinctively knew.

As Kammen and others have indicated, the writing of history is always a selective process and never without bias; each generation will ask new questions, based on its perspective and its special concerns. But, again quoting Kammen, "To be a local historian is to make a contribution that endures."

Local historians, like Miss Hemenway and her successors to the present day all over the world, face the same challenges, regardless of the changes in the societies in which they exist. There is still little money for local history, needs still overreach capacity, historical resources still are being lost at an alarming rate.

Local historians—amateurs and professionals alike—must persist in saving and interpreting their history, both for the benefit of present understanding and for that of the generations that will follow. If Miss Hemenway could succeed as well as she did, surely we can succeed, too, if we are willing to meet the challenges head on.

PAMELA J. BENNETT
President, American Association for State & Local History

7

F. W. Beers

Atlas of Rutland C?.
Vermont

1869

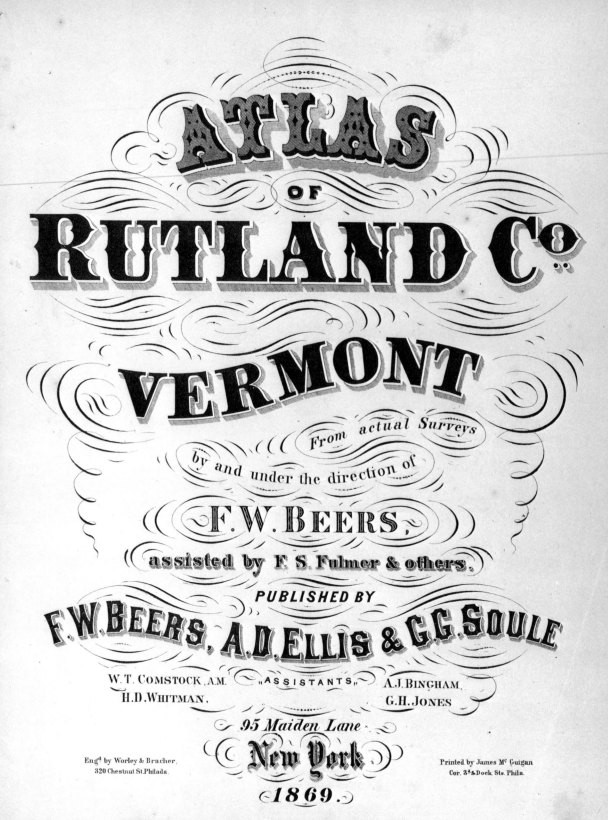

ATLAS

OF

RUTLAND Co.

VERMONT

From actual Surveys

by and under the direction of

F. W. BEERS,

assisted by F. S. Fulmer & others,

PUBLISHED BY

F. W. BEERS, A. D. ELLIS & G. G. SOULE

W. T. COMSTOCK, A.M.   "ASSISTANTS"   A. J. BINGHAM,
H. D. WHITMAN,   G. H. JONES

95 Maiden Lane
New York
1869.

Engd by Worley & Bracher,
320 Chestnut St. Philada.

Printed by James McGuigan
Cor. 3d & Dock Sts. Phila.

Entered according to Act of Congress in the year 1869 by Beers, Ellis & Soule, in the Clerks Office of the District Court of the United States in the Southern District of New York.

G EOGRAPHY is concerned with the spatial distribution of phenomena. Nothing expresses the essence of geography more than maps depicting such relationships at a particular time, a task admirably illustrated by the truly American 19th-Century phenomenon, the county atlas.

One of the most prolific producers of county atlases, Frederick W. Beers, is credited with compiling more than eighty county atlases—covering portions of ten states—during a career that spanned more than seventy years. Born at Berlin, Maryland, but long a resident of Brooklyn, New York, in 1858 he joined a cousin, Silas Beers, to work on his first county atlas, and he was still publishing such atlases in 1929, at the age of ninety, only four years before his death.

During the three decades following the Civil War, publication of county atlases reached their peak. Originally, single maps of counties and townships were prepared, to satisfy local demands. These maps were quite large (often drawn on a scale of one inch to the mile) and easily damaged. Thus, it was only natural to introduce county atlases—bound volumes containing a series of township maps—to render the maps more durable, as well as easier to carry and store.

Collection of township maps into an atlas format made it possible for a publisher to include pages of drawings of homes, places of business, municipal buildings, and landmarks—a pro-vision that allowed the publisher to raise the price of the volume and that helped to ensure sufficient sales to recover survey and publication costs. Thus, county atlases were not only useful records of properties at the time of atlas preparation, they were also good financial propositions for the surveyors and publishers. Some mapmakers amassed substantial fortunes.

No fewer than eight members of the Beers family were engaged in surveying and in producing county maps and atlases between 1855 and 1915. During the two decades following 1864, family members, singly or in cooperation, were responsible for the issuance of more than one hundred and twenty-five atlases, the majority of which centered on New England or the Middle Atlantic states.

Frederick and Silas Beers, after assisting in the production of maps for several New York counties, collaborated during the early 1860s in producing maps for additional counties in Pennsylvania and New Jersey. Following brief service in the Civil War, Frederick returned to county mapping again, doing work relating to Pennsylvania, New Jersey, and Michigan.

Between 1869 and 1878 Frederick Beers published atlases of thirteen of Vermont's fourteen counties. Only Essex County, in the northeast corner of the state, was not mapped by Beers—possibly because he did not feel that there were sufficient inhabitants or businesses there to make the probable return on the project worth the effort. In 1869 he produced atlases for Rutland, Bennington, Chittenden, Windham, and

Windsor Counties. Atlases for Addison County and (together in one volume) for Franklin and Grand Isle Counties appeared in 1871; for Washington, Caledonia, and Orange Counties in 1873, 1875, and 1877, respectively; and (again, published as a single volume) for Lamoille and Orleans Counties in 1878.

County atlases are of considerable interest, in and of themselves. They are often quite decorative, and they provide accurate information on the location of individual properties, as well as other useful data. In the case, for example, of Beers' Rutland atlas, the town maps typically carry "Directory" entries for local institutions and enterprises, professional and business persons, and prominent citizens. Also found within the volume are tables of statistics and distances and a listing of "the heights of all the important points in the valley of Quechee River and Eastern towns of Rutland Co." The atlas ends with pages devoted to lithographs depicting prominent structures and scenes from within the county.

To the geographer 19th-Century county atlases serve as cartographic "snapshots" of the layout of roads and towns, giving the locations of businesses, churches, residences, and other points of interest. When compared with similar maps produced at later dates, they yield information needed for studies of demographic, economic, political, or social change. They are basic to any understanding of local historical geography, and for that we will ever be indebted to individuals like F. W. Beers and his contemporary mapmakers, whether they were motivated by profit, service, or just love of geography.

JOHN R. MATHER
President, Association of American Geographers

8

G. G. Benedict

Vermont in the Civil War

1886–1888

VERMONT IN THE CIVIL WAR.

A HISTORY

OF THE PART TAKEN BY THE

VERMONT SOLDIERS AND SAILORS

IN THE

WAR FOR THE UNION,

1861-5.

By G. G. BENEDICT.

VOLUME 1.

BURLINGTON, VT. :
THE FREE PRESS ASSOCIATION.
1886.

IN 1853 George Grenville Benedict joined his father, George W. Benedict, in the management of the Burlington *Free Press*, and except for a year when he served with the Vermont volunteers in the Civil War, he was thereafter active in operations of the newspaper, becoming its editor-in-chief in 1866, a position he held until his death in 1907.

Benedict had been appointed state military historian in 1878, and it was in that role that he wrote *Vermont in the Civil War*. The work is a treasure of Civil War history. It takes the reader from Governor Erastus Fairbanks's proclamation announcing the outbreak of armed rebellion, and his response to President Abraham Lincoln's call for a regiment "for immediate service," through to the First Cavalry's presence at Lee's surrender at Appomattox Court House.

On April 5, 1865, Major General Godfrey Weitzel, who commanded all of the Union troops north of the Appomattox River, told Edward H. Ripley, commander of Vermont's Ninth Regiment: "I have sent for you, General Ripley, to inform you that I have selected you to take command in this city, and your brigade as its garrison. I have no orders further to communicate except to say that I want this conflagration stopped and the city saved. . . ." Thus, it was Ripley who was responsible for the preservation of the remains of the Confederate archives in Richmond.

Benedict, with the skill and instincts of an accomplished journalist, sums up the Vermont story. He writes of Vermont soldiers: "The history of the war cannot be written without frequent and honorable mention of them. A Vermont regiment was the first to throw up the sacred soil of Virginia into Union intrenchments. Vermont troops made the first assault upon a Confederate fortification. In almost every great battle fought in the succeeding years by the Army of the Potomac, Vermonters took an honorable part."

Vermont was indeed among the first in valour, sacrifice, and service in the Civil War. Vermont furnished well over 30,000 men for service in the army, navy, and marine corps during the Civil War, of whom 120 were black soldiers. More than 5,000 died as a result of battle wounds, disease, and other causes. (Some 350 died at Andersonville, the Confederate prison in Georgia.) Benedict stated, with more than a little justification, that in proportion to population, "Vermont had more of her sons killed in battle than any other Northern State, and gave to the cause of the Union more lives lost from all causes than any other State."

Vermont also has the distinction of having been the site of the northernmost engagement of the Civil War. It occurred on October 19, 1864, at St. Albans, just twenty miles south of the Canadian border. Led by Lieutenant Bennett H. Young, a young Confederate cavalryman from Kentucky, thirty Confederate soldiers (not in uniform, but all carrying or wearing some item of Confederate equipment, to ensure that, if captured, they would be treated as soldiers, not as ruffians or spies) straggled into the town, singly and in small groups beginning on October tenth. The raid began just a few minutes before three o'clock in the afternoon of the nineteenth, with St. Albans' three banks as the main objective. After robbing the banks they planned to burn the town.

The townspeople were incredulous and stunned when Young and his men identified themselves as Confederate soldiers come north in reprisal for General Philip H. Sheridan's depredations in the Shenandoah Valley of Virginia. However, when the initial shock wore off, the citizens of St. Albans sought weapons and began to fight back.

The Confederates failed in their attempt to burn the town, but fled to Canada with about $20,000. (This amount has been exaggerated to as much as $200,000.) One citizen was killed. Young and twelve of his men were captured, and they were held by the Canadian police in Montreal until December, when they were released.

Benedict ends his two-volume work with an eloquent commentary on the war: "Yet brute courage is not a very laudable quality, and military glory is surely not the highest glory. . . . It is because these Green Mountain bayonets were *thinking* bayonets; because the courage of these men was *manly* courage; because its underlying principle was devotion to *duty*; because the service was *patriotic* service, that it is worth commemorating. . . ."

RALPH G. NEWMAN
Founder, The Civil War Round Table

9

M. D. Gilman

*The Bibliography
of Vermont*

1897

X 1144.

W. P

THE

BIBLIOGRAPHY OF VERMONT

OR

A LIST OF BOOKS AND PAMPHLETS

RELATING IN ANY WAY

TO THE STATE.

WITH BIOGRAPHICAL AND OTHER NOTES.

PREPARED BY

M. D. GILMAN, Montpelier, Vt.

[WITH ADDITIONS BY OTHER HANDS.]

BURLINGTON : V
PRINTED BY THE FREE PRESS ASSOCIATION.
1897.

THIS book is one of those delightful, informative, eccentric, antiquarian constructs of the late-19th Century, prepared by devoted sons and daughters to honor their native places. Like other volumes of this nature, Gilman's bibliography grew out of the patriotic fervor generated by our national centennial of 1876 and is, as is Abby Maria Hemenway's *Vermont Historical Gazetteer*, a supreme example of its genre.

Marcus Davis Gilman was born in Calais, Vermont, in 1820. In 1845 he went to Chicago, where for the next twenty-three years he was engaged in a very successful mercantile business. He became a highly respected and leading citizen of that city, and while there he developed historical interests, becoming a book collector in the process. He and his family moved East in 1868, and in 1871 they returned to Vermont, to Montpelier, where the family settled into a large house adjacent to the capitol building.

Back in his home state, Gilman again involved himself in historical matters. He served from 1874 until 1881 as the librarian of the Vermont Historical Society, greatly increasing its collections during his tenure. Significantly, he used that central post to begin a comprehensive bibliography of printed materials pertaining to the state. Over the next fifteen years he compiled a list of such materials, annotating many of them. In the end, it numbered some seven thousand entries.

By January 1879, believing he had reached a point where publication of his material would be useful and could well elicit additions to his files, Gilman began publishing his findings, in eighty-nine installments that ran in the Montpelier *Argus and Patriot*. He continued work on the bibliography until his death in January 1889, fully expecting to publish it in a revised, comprehensive, and permanent form. Gilman's intentions were fulfilled in 1897, when the volume was published under the aegis of the State of Vermont, its legislature having voted to issue it—one copy to be given to each public library and town clerk's office. (The work was somewhat improved, edited, and seen through the press by George G. Benedict, editor of the Burlington *Free Press*, in whose printing office eight hundred copies of the bibliography were produced.)

Marcus Gilman's work was not to be rivaled until 1981, when the Committee for a New England Bibliography published *Vermont: A Bibliography of Its History* by T. D. Seymour Bassett, as the fourth volume in its series of guides to the history of the New England states. Even a century later, however, Gilman's work remains an essential source, because it contains scores of entries that fall outside the scope of Bassett's more closely defined compilation.

As the compiler of *Vermont Imprints 1778–1820*, I myself found the canvassing of Gilman's pages to be both essential and entertaining. In addition to recording much diverting information about Vermont books and their authors, the inde-fatigable Gilman recorded fully one-fourth of the pre-1801 Vermont imprints that were listed in my own compilation. This highly respectable achievement includes a number of interesting rarities, and his information is uniformly accurate. It is also clear that the compilers of Charles Evans's *American Bibliography* and Joseph Sabin's *Dictionary of Books Relating to America* made thorough use of it, well before my time. (After thirty years, there remain a few of Gilman's entries that I have not been able to verify; for example, "*A Vision*, of the Departed Spirit of Mr. Yeamans" [1800] is still a ghost.)

Harold G. Rugg was a 20th-Century counterpart of Gil-man. A Vermonter and long a librarian at Dartmouth College, he bequeathed his collection of Vermontiana to the Vermont Historical Society. The thousands of annotations in his own, interleaved copy of "Gilman" were of great help to me, as was his listing of local histories helpful to Bassett.

Gilman's bibliography is an invaluable guide for those who are interested in Vermont's past, as well as an incentive to explore little-known—or perhaps, even, unimportant—by-ways of that past. Present-day scholarly protocols often inhibit the inclusion of revealing and amusing anecdotes that make an author or a book come alive, and we are the poorer for it. So, we thank Marcus Gilman for accumulating the knowledge and harboring the ability to make his *Bibliography of Vermont* a prime volume in the canon of the historiography of the Green Mountain State.

MARCUS A. McCORISON
President, American Antiquarian Society

10

*A History of Vermont's
Maple Sugar Industry*

1912

A HISTORY OF
Vermont's Maple Sugar
Industry

PUBLISHED BY

VERMONT MAPLE SUGAR MAKERS'
ASSOCIATION

MOUNTED on a six-foot base atop the dome of the Vermont state house in Montpelier stands a majestic, fourteen-foot-high wooden statue of "Agriculture," both gracing and dominating the capitol structure. It constitutes a proud symbol, proclaiming not only to Vermonters, but also to all the world, that Vermont continues uniquely to be a rural and agricultural state.

Among Vermont's special and traditional pursuits in agriculture is the making of maple syrup and maple sugar. It is said that for centuries before the arrival of New England's first settlers, the American Indians had tapped the sugar-maple tree, which each year produces a flow of sap in response to the freezing nights and warm days that come in late winter and early spring—sap that, if boiled down, becomes a gloriously sweet syrup and then, if further boiled, a dark, crystalline sugar.

The early colonists soon copied the native inhabitants in this seasonal occupation, thus beginning what was to become and still is an important activity in New England, as well as in other parts of the country, wherever the sugar maple is found and climatic conditions are favorable to such enterprise. Today, the annual production of maple syrup in Vermont can be as high as five hundred thousand or more gallons.

The content of the 1912 pamphlet featured here, which is both heavily and fascinatingly illustrated, admirably fulfills the instructive promise of the title carried on its front cover, *A History of Vermont's Maple Sugar Industry*. There is an introductory page on "Vermont: Home of the Sugar Maple." (And, indeed, the sugar-maple tree was ultimately designated, by legislative act in 1949, to be Vermont's "State Tree.") Then, the main text is divided into several sections that are historical in their coverage or descriptive of various manufacturing processes, procedures, and apparatus.

Present, too, are: some pertinent verse, a half-dozen pages of recipes for using maple products, several advertisements (mainly of sugar-making equipment), and a list of more than one hundred members of the association that brought this publication into being.

Really, however, it is of course dairying that has over the years constituted Vermont's principal agricultural orientation. This has been true to the point that Vermont has long been described (sometimes teasingly and sometimes, I suspect, enviously) as a state with more cows than people—something that has not been true, though, for several decades now, decades during which Vermont has achieved new heights in productivity: doubling the yield per cow in the last thirty years and, thus, totalling well over two and a quarter billion pounds of milk annually. (No wonder that, effective April 22, 1983, the state legislature saw fit to designate milk as the official "State Beverage"—a recognition or distinction no other state has, to my knowledge, accorded its milk producers and dairy industry.)

With respect to animal husbandry, sheep raising has also been of particular significance to the state—ever since William Jarvis, U.S. Consul at Lisbon and Chargé d'Affaires for Portugal 1802–11, introduced into this country the celebrated Merino breed. And with sheep, too, in Vermont it has been a case of beasts of the field outnumbering, at times, the human population—for example, by as much as nearly a six-to-one ratio in the mid-19th Century. (It is rather touching to note that William Jarvis's monument, in a Weathersfield, Vermont, cemetery bears upon it, quite appropriately, a Merino sheep, carved in bas-relief.)

In addressing the subject of animal husbandry, one surely should not fail to make mention of the Vermont origins—which reach back to the 1790s—of that handsome, sturdy, and versatile creature, the Morgan horse.

History also reminds us, I might add, that it was a Vermonter, Justin Smith Morrill (until well into this century, incidentally, holder of the record for the longest span of unbroken Congressional service: twelve years in the U.S. House of Representatives and thirty-two years in the U.S. Senate), who in 1862 fathered this nation's single most important piece of legislation affecting agriculture: the "Land-Grant College Act," giving public lands to states and territories to enable them to establish "colleges for the benefit of agriculture and the mechanic arts"—legislation that led to the development, within our Union, of those collegiate institutions and of their vital research and extension services, which to this day are the very foundation of American agriculture, the most productive agriculture in the world.

But I cannot think of Vermont and agriculture without warm, vivid personal memories of that towering champion of both, George D. Aiken, a United States Senator from Vermont from 1941 until his retirement in 1975—a man who always gave his occupation as "Farmer," rather than "Senator," and who indeed preferred to be called "Governor" (he having held that office in Vermont for two terms before moving on to the Senate). He was a member of the Senate's Committee on Agriculture & Forestry during his entire tenure, including therefore my own time as United States Secretary of Agriculture.

In the early years of the 1960s, Senator Aiken and I on occasion had our differences—sometimes, even, sharp disagreements. (He once paid me the compliment of calling a comment I had made to the press "one of the most ridiculous and misleading statements that any Cabinet officer ever issued"!) Nonetheless, we both believed deeply in agriculture's importance to the nation, and we shared a commitment to a furtherance of its interests, nationally and internationally. I came to admire and respect the Senator and to rely on his advice. When he asked me to deliver the second annual lecture sponsored in tribute to him by the University of Vermont, I felt highly honored.

George Aiken not only made a major contribution to agriculture per se, but also to rural America, sponsoring important legislation to bring to the countryside some of the amenities that city-dwellers enjoy. He also reached out to the poor and hungry nationwide, by sponsoring the Food Stamp Program.

Within the U.S. Senate, fortunately, Vermont continues to have prominent representation of, as well as special concern for, agricultural interests. Patrick J. Leahy, who won election in succession to George Aiken, immediately joined the Senate's Agriculture Committee (now formally designated the Committee on Agriculture, Nutrition & Forestry). He has served thereon throughout the past sixteen years and is currently the committee's chairman.

Finally, for a further reflection — a further statement — of Vermont as essentially being of rural and agricultural character, one needs but to look at the state's official seal — originally

designed by Ira Allen in 1778 — whereon are featured: a pine tree (with, significantly, fourteen branches or limbs), a cow, sheaves of grain, woodlands, and (apparently) open fields or pastures and moving bodies of water.

ORVILLE L. FREEMAN
United States Secretary of Agriculture 1961–69

11

Lewis D. Stilwell

Migration from Vermont

1948

MIGRATION
from Vermont

by LEWIS D. STILWELL
Professor of History
DARTMOUTH COLLEGE

MONTPELIER
VERMONT HISTORICAL SOCIETY
1948

IN the foreword of his book *The Yankee Exodus*, Stewart H. Holbrook wrote: "My interest in migration from New England began some forty years ago, when I first became conscious of the many deserted hill farms in my native Vermont, and in New Hampshire where I also lived. The old cellar holes, the orchards being slowly throttled by encroaching forest, moved me deeply. I had a fairly good idea of what had gone into the making of those hill farms and homes; and the fact that they had been abandoned, after a century or more, seemed to me a great tragedy. It still does."

The scholarly study *Migration from Vermont* (issued separately in 1948, eleven years after its initial publication within the *Proceedings of the Vermont Historical Society*) is concerned with the subject of "migration" as it relates to but one of the six New England states. The objective of its author, Prof. Lewis D. Stilwell, was to answer a series of questions:

"How did people live and make a living in Vermont between the Revolution and the Civil War? Why did a great part of these people find it wise or necessary to leave Vermont? What sort of persons became emigrants . . . ? Where did these emigrants go, and how, and why? And what did these ex-Vermonters contribute . . . to the larger life of America?"

At the very outset Professor Stilwell makes the startling declaration, "No other state in the entire Union has sent forth so large a proportion of its people to aid in the establishment of newer commonwealths." And he goes on to indicate that "Even before Vermont itself was half settled, migration from Vermont began; and this migration continued and increased, until by 1860 . . . forty-two *per cent* of the natives of Vermont were living in other states."

Although of course, over the years, there were involved departures northward into Canada, as well as to states east and south, it was conspicuously a movement west: to central and upper New York; then, onward to Ohio, Michigan, Illinois, Indiana, and Wisconsin; next, farther westward still, beyond the Mississippi and the Missouri; finally, to the Pacific Coast itself. Early and late, Vermonters followed—seemingly with a vengeance—the dictum of Horace Greeley (himself a sometime resident of Vermont), "Go West, young man, go West." Thousands upon thousands of Vermont's young men did as the great editor advised. Preponderantly they were farmers, wanting more fertile lands and better growing conditions. But there were various other laborers, too, as well as artisans, merchants, clergymen, lawyers, physicians—all intent upon seeking new and greater opportunities.

Nor was it only men who ventured westward. There were also Vermont women—women who either accompanied or subsequently followed husbands, fathers, or other family members; and women, moreover, who proceeded on their own, many of them to be schoolteachers in frontier communities.

Regarding the overall character and motivation of these

people Stilwell says, "Vermonters were good pioneers for a purpose, but rarely pioneers for pioneering's sake."

My own home state has Vermont associations, surely, as elements of its history. There were, for example, Vermonters among the earliest settlers of Lawrence, Kansas—settlers who came as part of the great "Free Soil" effort within the Kansas Territory. And one, a boy just entering upon his teens when his family arrived at Lawrence in the mid-1850s, was within little more than two decades' time sitting in the U.S. House of Representatives, as a Congressman from Kansas. His name was Dudley C. Haskell.

There are Kansas communities with names that derive from Vermont towns that had originally been home to their first inhabitants. Burlington is an instance of such, its principal founder having hailed from what is now Vermont's largest city.

Professor Stilwell points out that by 1860 there were in Kansas (then on the very eve of statehood) over nine hundred native Vermonters—citizens helping to create yet another of our nation's "newer commonwealths," its thirty-fourth state.

But it is fitting, I believe, that as a member of the Landon family I should here express gratitude for the fact that the migratory nature of Vermonters, which the Stilwell volume so thoroughly chronicles for the period 1776–1860, had not by the Presidential-election year 1936 brought about a truly total depletion of the state's voting-age residents—and in particular those of Republican persuasion. My father would, I know, want me to reaffirm an appreciation of such.

NANCY LANDON KASSEBAUM
United States Senator from Kansas

12

Dorothy Canfield Fisher

Vermont Tradition

1953

Vermont Tradition

THE BIOGRAPHY OF AN
OUTLOOK ON LIFE

By DOROTHY CANFIELD FISHER

*The present contains nothing more
than the past. And what is found in
the effect was already in the cause.*
HENRI BERGSON

Boston
LITTLE, BROWN AND COMPANY

IT may appear odd that an outsider (an "outlander," as natives say) should proclaim his affinity with Vermont. An examination of my personal history, however, reveals that I have always been strongly attracted to the place. Others, too, have adopted it or arranged to have themselves adopted, the most illustrious case being that of Robert Frost, a Californian who identified himself with rural Vermont. There are precedents for such geographical choices or alliances. The Doge of Venice used to marry the Adriatic in a lavish ceremony. Frost united himself to Vermont by plowing, apple-picking, mending walls, and teaching school.

A Chicagoan for most of my life, I was born in the Province of Quebec and spent my early childhood just over the border along the St. Lawrence. Thus, I still respond strongly to the atmosphere, the vegetation, the chemistry, and the spirit of the Eastern woodlands. Illinois does not have anything like the same magnetic attraction for me, and if the connection should be partly imaginative, so much the better from my point of view.

Dorothy Canfield Fisher tells us that Quebec figured historically in the founding of Vermont, for when Montreal surrendered in 1760, ending the French and Indian War, some of the Colonials who served in the British army followed the rivers and trails of Vermont as they hoofed it back home. Later many of these militiamen returned as settlers. Americans who served in that campaign "answered to names now to be found on the voting lists of one or another Vermont town."

I remember that Mrs. Fisher, a prolific writer, contributed to magazines I read when I was very young. Names like *The Century*, *The Forum*, and *The Saturday Review of Literature* rise before me. And I can see now why a child of European immigrants, growing up in Chicago and eager to Americanize himself, would have been wrought upon, glamorized, and enchanted by what he read in those old magazines about the early history of the United States. Schoolchildren then were fascinated by Fenimore Cooper, Parkman, Washington Irving, and Hawthorne. In crowded, chaotic immigrant Chicago, Leatherstocking and Yankee farmers turned our heads. If Chicago was crowded and formless, New England was sparsely populated and its towns had a distinctive character. New Englanders were presented to us as silent, strong, reserved, and independent. We were to learn later from Thoreau, from E. A. Robinson, and from Frost himself that they were also neurotic and quietly desperate, but the fix was in, the early romantic attachment survived, the sophisticated revisions that came with maturity did not wipe them out. And there was, after all, some substance underneath the myths.

Mrs. Fisher's book, published almost half a century ago, proves that to us. "The life of Vermont men and women has always been colored by the absence of immense numbers of human beings," she writes. "Our relations with each other have been individual and personal." What a heavenly state of affairs, how delightful it is to think in the present urban mob scene of the absence of immense numbers. As for the individual and personal relations she speaks of, they have an almost utopian and melancholy effect on us. However, our nerves, like the coaxial or fiber-optic cables we read about, make it possible to strike a balance between disorder and tranquility. It is up to each of us to hold on to order and accommodate anarchy simultaneously. For this purpose Vermont is an ideal location.

Wandering in the woods as I often do, climbing over stone walls, I frequently come upon old foundations, heaps of brick, rusting farm machinery, and my mind, full of scenes from the Upper West Side of Manhattan or the slums of Chicago, makes room for local history (or archaeology). A hundred years ago there were pastures here. Now a scrubby second growth of new forest has taken over. Lilac bushes mark the driveways of vanished farms.

But Vermont is by no means one deserted settlement after another. It is fully up to date, industrial, electronic. Under the influence of television everyone is wised-up. Adolescents follow "The Grateful Dead" and other rock groups. The old ways, however, have not entirely disappeared. Vermonters still maintain their long reputation for Yankee alertness and manual skill. One of my neighbors generates his own electricity from a stream behind his house. A company in a nearby town manufacturers aged-looking barn board for people whose taste is for dens with an antique look.

The history of the state is a history of ingenious failed enterprises. Mrs. Fisher describes a few of them. As the old-fashioned subsistence farm produced no cash crops, she tells us, Vermonters of the last century did what they could with their meager resources. The home manufacture of potash thrived for a while, but the European discovery of new processes for the production of chemical lye put the ash-burners out of business. For some decades Spanish Merino sheep were bred here, but the state had no better luck with wool than with potash. Thus, one golden promise after another faded out. I recall that before the days of refrigeration, pond ice was a valuable export, as was Vermont stone. But the state produced no oil, no steel, no Detroit-style assembly lines. It is by no means a poor state. It has dairy farms, it has a considerable tourist industry, it has white-steepled villages. It has town meetings. Most significant of all, in my eyes, is its extraordinary beauty and its quietness. It sits inviolate just beyond the reach of the madness and anarchy of the cities. I find it ideal for the maintenance of sanity. Other parts of the country are thinly populated—the Dakotas, Montana, Wyoming, but there the open spaces are too open for my taste. I prefer the smaller horizons of Vermont.

When the birds wake you, you open your eyes on the massed foliage of ancient maples and hickories. After breakfast you carry your coffee out to the open porch. The dew takes up every particle of light. The hummingbirds chase away hummingbird trespassers from the fuchsias and the bee balm. Grass snakes come out of the rocks into the sun. The poplar leaves, when you narrow your eyes, are like showers of small change. And when you walk down to the pond you may feel what the Psalmist felt about still waters and green pastures.

SAUL BELLOW
Author and Teacher

13

Celebrating Vermont

1991

Celebrating Vermont:
Myths and Realities

Richard H. Saunders and Virginia M. Westbrook, exhibition curators

Edited by Nancy Price Graff

With essays by Nancy Price Graff & William N. Hosley, Jr.,
J. Kevin Graffagnino, and William C. Lipke

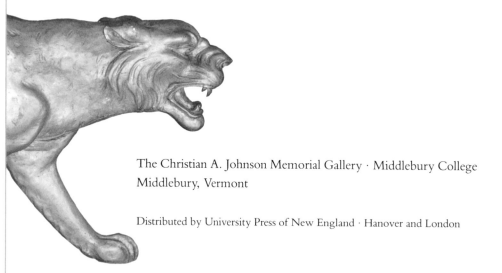

The Christian A. Johnson Memorial Gallery · Middlebury College
Middlebury, Vermont

Distributed by University Press of New England · Hanover and London

THE truth is that Vermont's people have leaned hard against the wind, from the beginning, often denied common measures of success. Perhaps this is why they are entitled to their myths.

It is especially gratifying that Vermont's "Myths and Realities" were taken up and focussed upon by Middlebury College's Christian A. Johnson Memorial Gallery and by the Bennington Museum during the period of the state's bicentennial observance, in the exhibition *Celebrating Vermont*—scheduled for showings at the Vermont Historical Society in Montpelier and at both Bennington and Middlebury. What were chosen for display are objects people made, used, and saved over time—objects kept, sometimes on purpose and sometimes because they were forgotten. This assemblage has been complemented, within the exhibition's catalogue, by three fine essays about the people who made and used myths, even as their own lives contradicted this fabricated wisdom.

The catalogue is more about myth than reality, although each defines the other. What are myths? By whom are they made, by whom kept, and for whom? Myths are long-lived. They are useful, defining character and perception; and they are rooted in truth. They are different from dreams, which are short-lived and sometimes unfulfilled.

We often link myth with folk culture, as may have been

true for those who found a hero in Ethan Allen. In Vermont's case, however, it appears that much of the myth-making was profitable image-making. It confirmed what others were asked to think about the state: fiercely independent and self-sufficient; blessed with Yankee ingenuity; a wilderness experience unspoiled by the urban; a 19th-Century Eden worth visiting; a 20th-Century Eden worth visiting.

But as the essayists who are featured here point out, reality was different. Roads, mills, newspapers, schools, towns, organizations, and up-to-date architecture were social phenomena, not mere acts of individuality. The decline of rural Vermont, the failure of shepherding to rescue farmers, the dissolution of the state's fledgling mills, and the inability of manufacturing to maintain a foothold—all speak of broken dreams that were far more apparent than myths to those who lived in Vermont. Today's singleness of image is belied by remarkable diversity of artistic expression, as well as by a tolerance for the eccentric.

How could myth and reality share the same space? We learn that myth was often a product intended for those outside the bosom of Vermont. Cash may have been sufficient motive for Allen's self-told story. Early developers needed the power of the agrarian myth to sell land. The boom in resorts between 1850 and 1920 depended upon delivering a matched set—advertising and a controlled experience—to the willing traveler. Myth-makers in the 20th Century, whose larger pallet includes the New England experience, continue to advance the "pastoral (mythic) and progressive (real) qualities that indeed make Vermont 'a special place.'"

It is not by accident that selected elements of Vermont's past remain visible. Memory has the help of the Division of Historic Preservation; it benefits from the Committee on Traditions and Ideals and the Vermont Commission on Country Life, not to mention tourism councils.

This catalogue's cover features Luigi Lucioni's oil painting "Village of Stowe," which confirms every visitor's image of Vermont. Its pages offer, along with paintings and sculpture and cabinetry and representations of architecture, friendly objects we all remember from a subliminal way-back past: a platform scale or a rod and reel, for example — or a cow weathervane from a barn (shot full of holes — I imagine by a boy with a good eye and a .22 rifle).

Sometimes symbols and myth have a way of becoming true. If Vermont is a state that time and fortune passed by too many times, it is also a state saved to remain "relatively rural, uncrowded, undeveloped, and out of step with the pace of the modern American technocracy." Perhaps society, inside and outside of Vermont, has come to value as real what was once only serviceable myth.

These reflections recall my own entry into Vermont from emptier Canada, through the town of Derby Line. Lodging was scarce, because of a women's softball tournament in Newport. Found at last, a bed-and-breakfast served nicely. I had always thought that Vermont would be just like the mythmakers said it was. And, you know, it really is.

ELLSWORTH H. BROWN
President, American Association of Museums

14

Vermont Life

Summer 1991

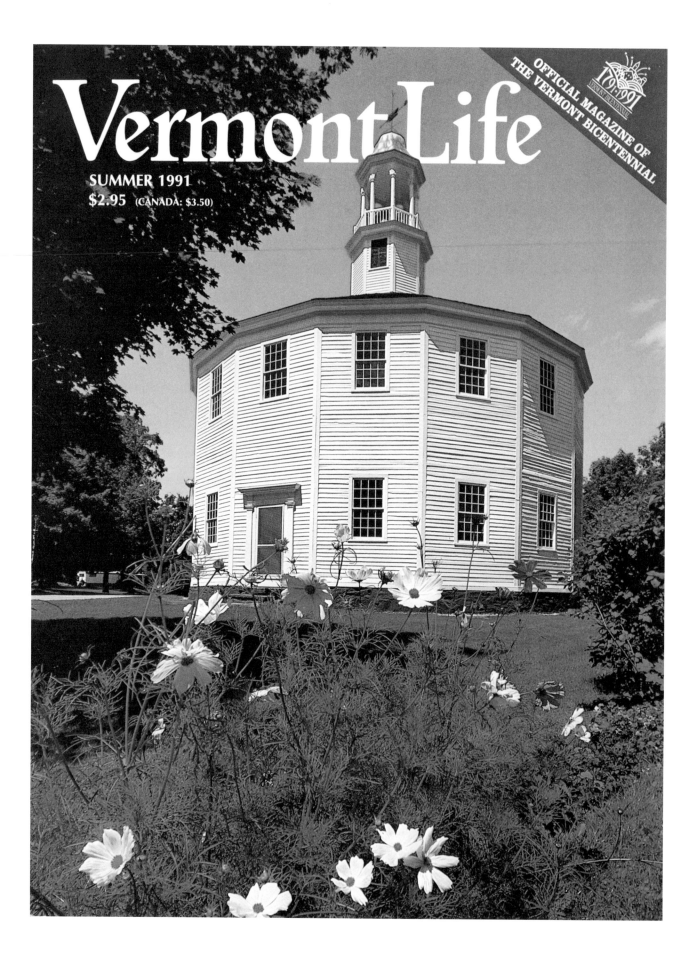

VermontLife

SUMMER 1991

$2.95 (CANADA: $3.50)

OFFICIAL MAGAZINE OF
THE VERMONT BICENTENNIAL

THE magazine *Vermont Life* is a commemoration of the nation's fourteenth state. It is appropriate (in my unbiased opinion) that the inside front cover of the publication's first issue was reserved for a governor. Forty-five years ago this autumn, Governor Mortimer R. Proctor greeted curious readers with these words of purpose and summation:

". . . If you are one of those who has not yet had an opportunity to know at first hand our beautiful countryside, the

[Volume I, Number 1]

friendliness of our people, and the 'Vermont way of Life,' this magazine will be a preview of what you may expect.

"If you are one of those who has already experienced the beauties of our Green Mountain State, this magazine will serve as a reminder at home of your pleasant hours in Vermont.

"If you are one of our own citizens, I know that the many articles and pictures which appear in this and succeeding issues will be a constant source of invaluable information regarding the industry and agriculture, history and government, art and architecture, of our own state. . . ."

Governor Proctor concluded his message by declaring that the magazine would "travel many places" and that it would, he felt confident, find a welcome wherever it went. Few politicians ever have made such an accurate prediction. Today, individuals from each of the fifty states and many countries around the globe eagerly await quarterly issues of *Vermont Life*.

Through the years, few periodicals in the public or private sector have established and maintained such a consistent level of distinction. *Vermont Life* remains a standard by which excellence is determined. As Vermont completes its bicentennial and enters its third century of U.S. statehood, the journal serves as an outstanding emissary and ambassador-at-large for the Green Mountain State.

On behalf of the nation's chief executives in the National Governors' Association, I extend on this special anniversary occasion our warmest greetings and our best wishes to all Vermonters, as well as the hope that Vermont will ongoingly enjoy God's richest blessings.

JOHN D. ASHCROFT
Governor of Missouri and
Chairman, National Governors' Association

FROM THE PROCLAMATION
OF MARCH 4TH, 1991

On March 4, 1791, the Republic of Vermont became the 14th State in our Union—the first to join the original thirteen. The Vermont State motto, "Freedom and Unity," is a fitting tribute to the history of the State and to the character of its people. . . .

Over the years, countless . . . Vermonters have made outstanding contributions to our country. . . .

Today, Vermonters take just pride in their heritage as a State committed to the ideals of freedom and unity. That heritage goes hand in hand with a rich legacy of growth and development. . . .

GEORGE BUSH
President of the United States

ACKNOWLEDGMENTS

The illustrations within this volume have derived from publications held by the following Vermont repositories—entries being by item number:

1 Dartmouth College Library once of "DRESDEN, STATE OF VERMONT"

2 Stewart-Swift Research Center, Sheldon Museum   MIDDLEBURY

3 Vermont Historical Society   MONTPELIER

4 Vermont Department of Libraries   MONTPELIER

5 University of Vermont Libraries   BURLINGTON

6 Dewey Library, Johnson State College   JOHNSON

7 Rutland Free Library   RUTLAND

8 St. Johnsbury Athenæum   ST. JOHNSBURY

9 Vermont Department of Libraries   MONTPELIER

10 Vermont Historical Society   MONTPELIER

11 Chaplin Library, Norwich University   NORTHFIELD

12 Starr Library, Middlebury College   MIDDLEBURY

13 Durick Library, St. Michael's College   WINOOSKI

14 Brooks Memorial Library   BRATTLEBORO

Except for #7, #13, and #14, which were reduced in reproduction, title pages and covers of the items featured are shown full size.

John Kenneth Galbraith's text, as included herein, draws on a chapter entitled "The Pleasures and Uses of Bankruptcy" that was originally published in his book *The Liberal Hour* (Boston: Houghton Mifflin, 1960).

Saul Bellow's final paragraph was adapted from the close of his article "The Good Place," featured in the July 1990 number of *Travel Holiday.*

The editors express gratitude to their colleague Stanley W. Brown, Curator of Rare Books at Dartmouth College, for assistance generously provided by him in connection with their preparation of this volume.

Published March 4th, 1992,
Vermont's 201st anniversary
of U.S. statehood.

Seven hundred seventy copies
have been printed at
The Stinehour Press
in the Northeast Kingdom
at Lunenburg, Vermont.
Designed by
Roderick Stinehour